Strategic Management of College Premises

Managing Colleges Effectively Series

Series Editor: Desmond Keohane, OBE, BA, FIMgt

A Guide to College Resource and Financial Management
Robert P. Lawrence

Increasing Effectiveness: A Guide to Quality Management
John Stone

The Funding Revolution: New Routes to Project Fundraising
Tom Roberts

Strategic Management of College Premises
Ken Ruddiman

Strategic Management of College Premises

Ken Ruddiman

Routledge
Taylor & Francis Group

LONDON AND NEW YORK

First published 1999 by RoutledgeFalmer

Published 2005 by Routledge
2 Park Square, Milton Park, Abingdon, Oxon OX14 4RN
605 Third Avenue, New York, NY 10017

Routledge is an imprint of the Taylor & Francis Group, an informa business

A catalogue record for this book is available from the British Library

Library of Congress Cataloging-in-Publication Data arè available on request

Cover design by Caroline Archer

Typeset in 12/14pt Garamond by
Graphicraft Limited, Hong Kong

Every effort has been made to contact copyright holders for their permission to reprint material in this book. The publishers would be grateful to hear from any copyright holder who is not here acknowledged and will undertake to rectify any errors or omissions in future editions of this book.

ISBN 13: 978-0-7507-0966-8 (pbk)

Contents

List of Tables and Figures

Introduction

Following incorporation and the merger in 1992 of Sheffield's six former Further Education colleges into one city–wide operation — making The Sheffield College the largest Further Education institution in Europe — it became clear that of the many major management tasks facing the new college, one of the most pressing was the need to completely review the overall provision of accommodation.

Many of our buildings were in a very poor state of repair, others were being under utilized, and it was clear that a wholesale review of the College's estate was essential. Although we knew that the process would be long and complicated, the two years we spent on planning a way forward raised many issues which we had not foreseen.

This book uses our experience of devising and implementing an accommodation strategy to draw out some general guidelines and advice which we hope will be of use to other colleges undertaking a similar task. Clearly, each set of individual circumstances will require a slightly different approach, but we believe there are many areas of common ground.

Ken Ruddiman,
Principal and Chief Executive
The Sheffield College

Chapter 1

Why Develop an Accommodation Strategy?

The dynamic environment in which further education operates means that an estate which met a college's needs even a decade ago could be quite inadequate today. Growing customer expectations, demographic changes, increasing curriculum-led demands, competition from other providers, and developing new technology are just some of the elements which may necessitate change. Premises which were built years ago to meet the training needs of heavy industry may need radical redevelopment to meet the demands of today's more technologically advanced business environment. College sites which were established to serve a local community may no longer be needed if much of that community has relocated, and many college premises may just be suffering from the ravages of time and under investment.

Although there may be differing reasons why colleges choose to develop a new accommodation strategy, there are a set of key objectives which can be usefully applied in devising an appropriate way forward, including:

- To provide a good quality environment within which students and staff can find appropriate facilities which promote their own objectives and the goals of the institution;

- To pursue excellence rather than physical size;

- To streamline and co–ordinate provision, taking into account the need of the various communities and neighbourhoods served by the college;

- To promote access by providing welcoming, safe and inspiring environments and to provide better facilities appropriate to supporting more flexible learning patterns, e.g. learning resource centres;

- To ensure that the institution's financial resources are directed towards its strategic goals, and not diverted to supporting inappropriate or unsuitable accommodation.

Whatever the scale of the changes required, they may take some time to bring to fruition. Given the constantly changing nature of the Further Education sector in meeting the needs of local business and the community, it should also be recognized that a successful accommodation strategy must contain a high level of flexibility.

The Sheffield College

The Sheffield College is the largest further education institution in the country, with more than 30,000 enrolled students. When the College began its accommodation review, its estate — inherited from the local authority on incorporation — comprised some 17 freehold sites, over a million square feet of accommodation (104,000 square metres), and 96 acres of land. In addition the College had a network of over 100 neighbourhood properties which were licensed or leased, usually from the local authority.

In the summer of 1994, The Sheffield College undertook a major premises review through the vehicle of an accommodation strategy. This was both a necessary step in the advancement of the College estate, and a requirement of the Further Education Funding Council (FEFC). A report, based on the outcomes of the study, was put before the governing body in the autumn of 1994 and was accepted as a statement of principle, subject to detailed investigations and consultation. The report was also accepted by the FEFC who acknowledged the accommodation strategy as a sound basis for estates planning.

Given the size and complexity of the College, the accommodation strategy was a major piece of work. Producing the report helped the College focus on the need for estates action and, in particular, in dealing with key issues such as inefficiency and low quality. However, the provision of premises affects all aspects of College life, and the community it serves, and a consensus was therefore reached that, before the College implemented any projects, it should consider the wider effects of any action. In particular, detailed attention to areas such as consultation and curriculum was considered to be vital to the future success of the strategy.

Chapter 2

Assessing What You've Got

The first decision to be made once the need for an accommodation review has been accepted is how to gather the information you need to provide a clear and detailed picture of where you are now. Perhaps, most importantly, you need to decide who will gather that information. Will you use existing staff, or will you employ external consultants? Colleges are also expected to provide a great deal of information on their estate to the FEFC, but many struggle with that requirement, owing to a lack of adequate resources available to provide the level of information and detail required.

Before making that decision, it is important to consider the pros and cons of each approach:

	External consultants	**In house staff**
Cost	More expensive	Cheaper
Time available	Can employ to work more or less full time	May have to fit work around existing full-time workload
Knowledge	Will not necessarily have background knowledge which could help them fulfil task	Existing knowledge of college and its premises could save time on job

Objectivity	Are likely to be objective as they have no stake in the future shape of the college	May not be entirely objective as they have a stake in the future shape of the college
Training and development	Specialist consultants are likely to already have expertise in the relevant area, and any training and development needs will be their own responsibility	Investment in training and development may be time consuming and expensive

Table 2.1: Consultants v. college staff reviews

Working with Consultants

Working effectively with consultants is a skill in itself, and one which needs to be fine tuned if maximum benefit is to be gained from the investment. To make effective use of consultants, the client must have a very clear and accurate understanding of their own requirements, so that the consultant can be effectively briefed to deliver the desired result. Bringing in external consultants can be useful to sow the seeds of change, as often a suggestion from an outsider may be considered, when a similar one from an insider could be considered politically unacceptable. An external consultant can also help to start the process of cultural change, which might be much more difficult to do from inside the organization. The appointment of a consultant can also help an organization to focus very clearly on its objectives, and the consultant can bring objectivity to sensitive areas, such as people's working environments or job security.

Choosing a Consultant

The following issues are amongst those which should be considered when choosing a consultant:

- Does the individual or company have good standing and experience in their particular field?

- Do they have a detailed knowledge of the sector or industry in which you are working, and can they advise you on other specialist input required?

- Does the company employ particular individuals with detailed knowledge and experience of what you are trying to achieve?

- Are the people you will be working with people that you can get on with and, most importantly, trust? After all, you will actually be handing over quite a lot of responsibility to them, and it is important that you feel confident about doing this;

- What is their fee for the work, and what exactly does this cover? Naturally, you will be looking for a cost effective proposal which offers value for money, **but it is important to bear in mind that, in an accommodation strategy, the consultant's fee is likely to be a small percentage of the overall cost**.

- Is the company stable, and can it offer an ongoing commitment at a high level to your project?

Writing a brief to appoint a consultant is quite exacting and it is important to get it right if you are going to achieve your objectives without going over budget. If no-one in your organization has much experience of appointing consultants, it would be worth seeking advice from someone who has.

Space and Utilization

Utilization Survey

Before deciding what amount and type of accommodation may be required for the future, you need to develop a clear understanding of what is happening now.

Firstly, you must establish the basis for your survey, for example:

- What assumptions are you making about hours per week usage, e.g. a 40 hour week, based on 9am–5pm, 5 days per week? The DES Standards of Utilization look for rooms being in use for 80 per cent of the available time, with the available time, set by the FEFC, considered to be 40 day-time hours, e.g. 9am–5pm, Monday to Friday.

- How many students are there during each one–hour period within every teaching space — thus giving you the number of 'student hours'?

- Utilization can be measured against the theoretical number of workplaces within the room, which could be calculated using the Department of Education and Science *Building Bulletin 37* space standards. Capacity is assessed on FEFC figures, so for a general classroom, a provision of $1.8m^2$ per student is made.

Whilst these standards were devized for new build projects they are considered the most accurate standards available.

Once the data has been gathered — preferably over a typical week of college activity — the results can be expressed as a 'Utilization Factor', which is calculated as follows:

$$UF = \frac{Demand}{Supply} \quad or \quad \frac{\text{'Student Contact Hours'}}{\text{Workplaces} \times \text{hours available}}$$

(Where 'Student Contact Hours' is the number of students counted attending a one–hour lesson during the week.)

Alternatively, the Utilization Factor can be expressed as follows:

UF = Room Utilization × Seat Utilization, where Room Utilization represents the percentage of hours a room is in use, and Seat Utilization represents the percentage of seats in use when the room is in use.

The theoretical number of workplaces calculated from the floor area may differ from that practically available depending on fixed furniture layout etc.

Utilization Survey and Future Targets

Armed with the results of your utilization survey, you can begin to plan target levels of utilization for the future.

Historically, it has been suggested that a target overall Utilization Factor of 64 per cent would be a reasonable standard to

Category	Description	m2/WP
1	Lecture Theatres	1.0
2	General Teaching	1.8
3	Information Technology	2.7
5	Laboratories	3.0
6	Art & Design/Drawing offices	3.2
7	Large scale Art and Design/Workshops with benches/Home Economics	4.5
8	Catering/Hairdressing	6.5
9	Welding/Motor Vehicle/Installation trades/Large Machinery	7.5

Table 2.2: Space norms for other types of provision

achieve. This was on the basis that teaching spaces ought to be in use 80 per cent of the time and, when in use, they ought to be on average 80 per cent full.

$$\text{Utilization Factor} = \text{Room Utilization} \times \text{Seat Utilization}$$

$$= 80\% \times 80\% = 64\%$$

However, it is generally recognized that, particularly with regard to specialized teaching spaces, 64 per cent is unrealistic. A range of specialized teaching spaces is invariably required in order to teach a particular course, and yet the enrolment numbers on that course may lead to only low levels of utilization (see Table 2.2). In these circumstances, colleges may wish to consider the viability of certain courses. It must be recognized, though, that the more specialist the teaching spaces, the lower the realistic utilization level.

The Sheffield College Experience

Within the Sheffield College a utilization survey was carried out, and this demonstrated an average Utilization Factor of 22 per cent. This average masked quite substantial differences between centres, with the highest Utilization Factor at 33 per cent and the lowest at 17 per cent.

Following the results of the survey, the College decided that, in the medium term, it would be realistic to aim to double levels of utilization from 22 per cent to around 44 per cent. This 44 per cent assumed no growth in the number of 'contact hours', and any increase in demand will result in a higher utilization.

Recognizing the different utilization potential of varied types of teaching spaces, the College decided to apply a sliding scale in terms of targets to different categories of teaching spaces. It was calculated that the following targets would result in an overall figure of 44 per cent:

Categories 1–3:	General Teaching spaces	47 per cent
Categories 4–6:	Small scale specialized spaces	37 per cent
Categories 7–9:	Large scale specialized spaces	34 per cent

These figures are only targets (which are most easily applied to new build projects) and it was recognized that certain factors would lead to slightly lower levels of utilization. Three principal factors are:

The College's curriculum plan

Inevitably, the proposed curriculum plan was influenced by the need to locate courses on a needs/marketing basis. Certain retained existing centres do not have sufficient students within the plan to generate the target levels of utilization.

Course briefings

The College consultants and senior managers carried out lengthy consultations/briefing sessions with all course leaders, and in certain circumstances, a case was established for a greater amount of space than could be justified by space norms alone. This was particularly true where activities requiring larger than average amounts of space were to be relocated. Ultimately, such 'special treatment' will require review, following further detailed briefings. However, where a reasonable case appeared to exist, it was considered better to cost the additional area for inclusion in the investment plans.

Pragmatism

It seemed unrealistic to expend significant monies to reorganize existing specialist spaces for modest reductions in overall space. Therefore, many existing spaces remain unaltered, despite their utilization levels being below target.

Overall, following careful analysis of its estate, and significant research into suitability, condition, areas, utilization and the need for new facilities, the results of the Sheffield College's analysis of its accommodation showed the following:

- The majority of the accommodation was reasonably well suited to its purpose;

- The condition of properties was variable, but many post–war buildings were rather rundown as a result of inadequate long term maintenance, and were at the end of their design lives;

- Utilization of space was not good, although variable. Typically, detailed utilization rates were about one third of their ideal target;

- The College had a wide range of opportunities to attend to its estate problems, including disposals, development and overhaul of the administration system. However, the estate still had a number of constraints, not least the town planning context;

- Changing educational patterns and growth in student numbers had resulted in deficiencies of a variety of accommodation types, particularly learning centres. However, research showed that this need, together with student growth, could still be accommodated within a substantially reduced estate.

Chapter 3

Curricular Assessment

Providing the right kind of premises, of appropriate quality and in the right geographical locations to deliver the required curriculum in the most efficient, effective and economical way is the ultimate aim of any accommodation strategy. However, this straightforward statement conceals the complexities behind reaching an optimum solution.

Many colleges have inherited a range of premises which may no longer be appropriate to meet the needs of today's curriculum. For example, large scale engineering workshops may need replacing with smaller units equipped with the latest in high technology; libraries may need expanding and developing into learning centres, and new methods of learning, such as distance and open-learning packages also have an effect on the type of accommodation a college requires.

Many college premises are simply suffering from the effects of old age. Buildings erected in the 1960s are now beginning to show signs of severe deterioration, and the costs of putting that right could be prohibitive. Rapid changes are also occurring within the marketplace, with increasing numbers of employers preferring delivery of vocational curriculum in the workplace — a significant change which will affect the day-release market. It is also widely recognized that in some vocational curriculum areas, delivery of the practical skills in the workplace is the most desirable way of addressing that element of the curriculum. However, some companies will still look to colleges to provide such opportunities through concentrated and modern resources.

Before making any firm decisions on the way forward, it is vital to have a clear picture of the college's curriculum plans and what accommodation will be required for delivery, with flexibility built in to take account of the rapidly changing environment and its effect on the demand for training and education.

DETERMINING THE CURRICULUM STRATEGY

There are three stages:

1   Determine the college's curriculum strategy in relation to distribution; Establish principles for curriculum distribution across the college's area of activity, and for curriculum mix within college centres (discussed in this chapter);

2   Examine the feasibility of the proposed options (discussed in Chapter 4);

3   Use 1 and 2 to shape final decisions about curriculum distribution and hence your accommodation strategy.

Stage 1: The College's Curriculum Strategy

Before making any attempt to relocate any curriculum provision, it is important to establish or re–establish the college's guiding principles in curriculum distribution. A number of questions need to be considered at this stage:

Curriculum distribution across college's area of activity

- What is the college's Mission?

- Is the curriculum driven by market needs only, or are there wider issues to be considered, such as equality of opportunity and the college's role in catering for educational needs in both the social and economic sense?

- What are the accommodation and resources implications of the proposed curriculum strategy?

- Is it possible to concentrate resources for the delivery of vocational advanced level studies?

- How many delivery points are required to meet the volume and distribution of demand?

- Is it possible to cluster delivery to maximize efficiency whilst still meeting customer need — e.g. on a north/south basis?

- Does your college wish to create a sixth-form centre or monotechnic, or do you want to maintain a mixed curriculum — in terms of levels, vocational and academic, gender and age groups — at all main centres?

- Is the opportunity for students to work with others from different generations and groups considered an important element of your curriculum?

- Do you aim to achieve parity of esteem for all types of provision — e.g. vocational, academic and levels (Higher Education and foundation)?

- What are the strategic advantages of the location of all main centres and how can you maximize the benefit of those advantages to users and potential users?

Curriculum mix across centres

- Should all main centres have core elements, such as A–level, GCSE, Adult Basic Education and community programme provision, or should centres specialize?

- Would it make sense to put vocational Intermediate and Advanced provision in the same centre?

- What sort of provision should there be in each centre to take account of the particular characteristics of the local catchment area?

- Is provision for students with Learning Difficulties and Disabilities to be integrated into mainstream provision at all centres, rather than dealt with as a separate issue.

Changing Market Conditions and Demands

Having considered the ideal principles for curriculum distribution and mix, and prior to considering options, it is important to develop a clear picture of key changes in the current market. Issues for consideration include:

Population growth and housing trends

- Where are the highest levels of young people under 15 within the college's area of activity?

- Where are new housing developments currently being built, and what are the trends for the next ten years?

Feeder schools and sixth form provision

- Do the local feeder schools currently have sixth form provision or, if not, are they planning to introduce it?

- Should the college take steps to structure its provision in line with market demands, thus rendering the 'demand' for additional sixth forms unnecessary?

External pressure for more efficient and effective use of resources

- Can your curriculum strategy and its consequent effect on accommodation strategy offer your college a real opportunity to strategically rationalize its programme to match market needs and to achieve higher efficiency and effectiveness?

- Can you avoid duplication through concentration of specialist provisions and facilities and by introducing more efficient timetabling processes, thus allowing you to meet external demands for more efficient and effective use of resources without compromising your curriculum principles?

Significant market changes and demands in terms of curriculum content and delivery

- Rapid changes are taking place in the market place. A major change is that increasing numbers of employers now prefer delivery of vocational curriculum in the workplace — a significant move which is already particularly affecting the day–release market. Do your planned curriculum and accommodation strategies take adequate account of this development?

- It is also widely recognized that in some vocational curriculum areas, delivery of the practical skills in the workplace is the most desirable way to address that part of the curriculum, but while reasonable sized companies can offer opportunities on company premises, smaller companies will remain dependent on colleges to provide such opportunities with concentrated and modern resources. Do your plans contain the flexibility to meet these differing demands?

Government-introduced changes

- How will the new Modern Apprenticeships affect your future full–time numbers?

- The Competitiveness White Paper implies that many other organizations will soon have direct access to FEFC funding — how will this impact on the college's activities and student numbers?

The Sheffield College Experience

The Sheffield College accommodation strategy identified three principles on which any proposed rationalization should be based:

- Specialist space and, therefore, specialist vocational facilities should occur only once in the city in order to maximize investment and development;

- Each main centre should include a core of amenities and facilities which will reflect and support curriculum strategies including learning resource centres and the use of information technology;

- The strategy should focus primarily on the College's freehold estate and, therefore, the majority of provision in the neighbourhood centres would not be changed.

The College's Mission Statement clearly specifies that it exists to **stimulate**, **encourage** and **respond**. This indicates that the College will not be driven by identified market needs only, but will work proactively to stimulate aspiration, interest and commitment in participation of education and training at all levels and in all parts of Sheffield. Therefore, it is vital that the curriculum distribution reflects the social and economic needs of the city, and it should therefore include the following elements:

- The College emphasizes the value of mixture of curriculum at all main centres — in terms of levels, vocational and academic subjects, gender and age groups. When considering curriculum distribution, due attention needs to be paid to avoid the creation of sixth form centres or monotechnics, in image or reality. Students' rounded social experience is regarded as an important element of the curriculum;

- The strategic locations of all main neighbourhood centres should be fully developed by offering a curriculum which consciously creates benefits to current and potential users of that centre;

- All community provisions should be located and delivered at times suitable to achieve maximum accessibility to the majority of community user groups;

- Any planned change in premises use or relocation will take into account the support needs of the student population — both able-bodied students and students with disabilities — and the underpinning teaching and learning strategies;

- Multi-skills workshops will provide a resource for students from a range of curriculum areas to develop generic practical skills in intermediate/foundation vocational areas;

- Demand for childcare continues to grow. Existing 25 place units at main centres are already too small for current demand and therefore consideration of increasing facilities will be made;

- Facilities available for open access resources, supported self study/resource based and open learning reflect the curriculum areas offered in each centre and area they serve;

- A significant programme of learning resource centre development is a major part of the College's curriculum strategy and, along with the increasing use of information technology, will be reflected in premises proposals.

Chapter 4

Financial Implications

Stage 2: Examining the Feasibility of Proposed Options

Once you have gathered all the data relating to the current curriculum, future proposals, and internal and external demands, you will be in a position to draw up a number of options, which may range from doing nothing at all to a compete overhaul of all your premises. Issues for consideration at this stage include financial assessment and sources of finance.

Financial Assessment

First of all, you will need detailed costings on each of the options, and identification of possible sources of funding. Obviously, until you make a final decision on the shape of your accommodation strategy, certain funding components will remain unknown — for example, grant applications will always be uncertain until final confirmation is given — but the realistic possibilities for funding improvements and new developments must be considered at this stage.

Sources of Finance

Virement of Hunter Funds

One possibility for funding is the virement of Hunter Funds allocated to properties now earmarked for closure to fund the new works programme. The Further Education Funding Council has indicated that in certain circumstances it would be prepared to support the virement of such Funds to support an accommodation strategy, on the following basis:

- That the projects allocated for virement fall within the accommodation strategy and its subsequent development;

- That the college undertakes to remove the problem source for which the Hunter Funds were originally allocated;

- That the funds allocated for virement fall below the remaining unspent available pool of 1A and 1B monies allocated to the college;

- That the projects allocated for virement are regarded as good value for money according to Funding Council criteria.

As projects are brought forward for implementation, the college should seek the FEFC's approval for the viring of Hunter Funds. At this stage, the college must be able to demonstrate that it has eliminated sufficient risk and uncertainty to confirm that the project meets the Council's value for money criteria, or else be able to demonstrate that the base costs are consistent with site specific abnormals accounting for the difference.

Colleges may also wish to seek specific guidance from the Funding Council on the following:

- That the Hunter Funds may substantially be drawn down against construction budgets, thereby enabling you to minimize your borrowings and maximize cash flow;

- That Hunter Funds may be drawn down in lump sums, rather than in support for borrowing as encouraged by Circular 95/25. It is important to seek confirmation that in doing so, you would not prejudice bids for capital support under Circular 95/25.

Although it certainly seems possible to make effective use of Hunter Funds in this way, it is important to engage in ongoing discussions with the Funding Council, to ensure that any alterations to your accommodation strategy do not result in a withdrawal of support for this type of financing. It is also important to note that the funds are not transferred to the college in advance of construction, but are drawn down against stage payments as approved virement projects proceed.

Disposal receipts

Another substantial funding component may be the receipts gained from the disposal of redundant properties. When planning your accommodation strategy, it is important to consider how much you may be able to realise through sales. Clearly, the market value of your redundant properties will be significantly affected by the local planning context, and it may be possible for you to make representations to the local authority to alter these.

In the **Sheffield College's** case, the local authority's Unitary Development Plan enquiry was ongoing during the time that the College was planning its accommodation strategy, and it was clear that, particularly in the cases of the planned disposal of two main sites, alterations to the proposed acceptable uses on those sites could make a significant difference to the amount the College would be able to raise on disposal. Because of this, the College employed a firm of planning consultants to represent its case at the enquiry. Although it is felt that the representations were well made and the enquiry went smoothly, at the time of writing the College is still awaiting the Inspector's report.

The College chose to use a firm of external consultants in this instance because it felt it had neither the time nor the expertise in house to maximize the potential benefit of making representations to the enquiry, and the costs of doing so were felt to be far outweighed by the possible gains should the representations be successful. The type of gains which the Sheffield College hoped to make achieving beneficial planning consent:

Expected disposal value	Alternative disposal value with beneficial planning consent
£1,989,000	£3,439,000

Because of the medium term uncertainty of challenging the local planning framework, it is obviously prudent to plan financially on the basis of the existing framework, with any changes achieved being seen as an added bonus.

College reserves

Should your college be in the position of having reserves which can be utilized to support the accommodation strategy, then this is clearly an option worth considering.

Contribution from revenue funding

Similarly, if the college is operating with a surplus, it may be possible to support some of the accommodation strategy through the use of revenue funding.

At the time of planning its accommodation strategy, the **Sheffield College** was operating with a deficit, but had submitted a forecast to the FEFC, which showed recovery over a short period, and an operating surplus by the end of the decade. Inevitably, this forecast addressed the issue of overall staffing levels and costs, many of which were then brought into sharper focus as result of the accommodation strategy and the prospective closure of certain sites with staffing transfer implications.

Although the College's revenue finance could not support the accommodation strategy in the short term, it was hoped that the successful implementation of the recovery plan would lead to a surplus in future years, which could be best utilized for the completion of the accommodation strategy, or for achieving certain desirable projects, which have not been included in the plans to date as they have not been considered absolutely essential.

While undertaking small scale refurbishment projects, the College normally considers a part of the works to be capital expenditure, and a part of the works to be refurbishment, assessed as revenue expenditure. Although a number of the accommodation strategy projects are quite small, and substantially refurbishment, the College has considered all projects to be capital expenditure. This is because the projects form part of a total programme designed to substantially rationalize the estate and, irrespective of their cost or nature, they are integral to this overall programme. The College's auditors and independent valuers will be consulted on an ongoing basis, and before any construction project is undertaken.

Grants

Colleges may be eligible to apply for grant assistance, both on account of its activities and its location. Grant sources for which colleges may be eligible include European Regional Development Fund (ERDF), RECHAR, Department of the Environment (DOE) funding and, for some projects, lottery funding. There may also be the possibility of funding from charitable foundations.

If you do not have a member of staff who is a grant specialist, it may be worth considering the use of a consultant in this area, as a detailed understanding of the grant regimes and how to maximize success rates could prove invaluable. Before finalizing your accommodation strategy, it is important therefore to assess possible grant sources, the maximum level of support and realistic chances of success.

However, it has to be recognized that many of the grant regimes have very strict guidelines, and applying for grant funding may in itself dictate the nature of some of your proposals. For example, a college might be successful in obtaining support for an IT suite to support re-training for the long-term unemployed. While such facilities may be compatible with other college uses, such facilities would have to be at least partially delineated and could not be taken as a substitute for other college uses.

VAT Planning

Although not strictly a funding source, the opportunity to defer VAT cannot be overlooked. Your accommodation strategy is likely to be expensive, and it would seem prudent to take any opportunity to spread these costs. It is reasonable to take sensible measures to defer or avoid VAT payments, if these fall within conventional VAT practise.

To avoid paying unnecessary VAT most efficiently it is likely that the services of a good VAT consultant will be required. It is a very specialized area and it is unlikely there will be anyone in house with the appropriate detailed knowledge. These can be found in the following ways:

- Recommendations;

- Through the main accountancy bodies, such as the Chartered Institute of Public Finance Accountants; the Institute of Chartered Accountants; or the Chartered Institute of Certified Accountants;

- Approaching, any of the major accountancy firms;

- Through tendering.

The most important element of successful VAT planning is to plan ahead. From the outset, you need to identify any opportunity to save or defer VAT, as it is often difficult to do so retrospectively. Therefore, your VAT consultant or in house expert needs to be involved from the beginning of the process. Many VAT consultants will take on contracts on a contingency basis, i.e. if they don't save you anything, you don't have to pay them.

There are two main routes for legitimate avoidance of VAT, which can be beneficial for colleges:

1 Using the legislation to get items zero-rated. This route is particularly relevant when planning your accommodation strategy, as it can apply to new buildings. For example, if you have less than 10 per cent of fee paying students using a new building, you may not have to pay VAT. Therefore, it could make sound financial sense to try and locate all 16–19-year-olds together, or with those on free courses. However, this solution is not always as simple as it might appear in terms of wider college objectives, timetabling etc. You may set up what appears to be a workable system, but then find it altered by circumstances. For example, you may have an A-level class which is normally for 16–19-year-olds, but low numbers could result in you opening it up to fee-paying adults, which in turn could take you over the 10 per cent limit for the building. In spite of potential difficulties though, this route is worth active consideration in your early planning phase.

2 Putting appropriate structures in place which avoid or reduce the amount of VAT you may have to pay. This may involve the use of subsidiary companies. For example, many colleges have set up separate but wholly owned companies to carry out certain areas of work, particularly in the business training area. This enables

them to reclaim VAT paid, putting them on a level playing field with other training providers on the open market. The company operates as a separate legal entity, carrying out contracts on behalf of the college, and the college recharges the company for staffing and management time.

Before entering any scheme, it is vital that you have approval. Your VAT consultant should check this. When agreeing a contract with your VAT consultant, it is wise to include a clause establishing that, if there are any problems with Customs and Excise, the agreed fee covers any costs incurred through going to tribunal and beyond. If your VAT consultant is confident about the scheme they are proposing, they should be confident enough to assume the risk.

The other major issue to consider is your long–term relationship with your tax inspector. Generally, it is better to be upfront, share your plans with them and consider any concerns they may have. If you work closely with your tax inspector, you are much less likely to face unexpected problems later on.

To summarize, VAT planning can be an extremely effective way of saving money. VAT planning on just one element of The Sheffield College's accommodation strategy released an additional £1/4 million for investment, and a total of £3/4 million was saved in just over a year. There are certainly many savings to be made, but many are missed because the possibility is considered too late in the process, and it may not be possible to do anything retrospectively. There is also a danger that decision–making can become VAT driven, and it is important that the right balance between saving VAT and the wider aims of the college is achieved.

Capital support from the Further Education Funding Council

Circular 95/25 and 96/11 sets out the FEFC's strategy for capital funding and the terms under which it will consider funding bids. Each funding bid must be assessed on its merits and therefore it is difficult to identify an overall level of support which might be forthcoming from the FEFC.

Table 4.1 below shows the assessment made by the **Sheffield College** of possible levels of FEFC support for each individual element of its accommodation strategy. The College's ALF at the time of planning the accommodation strategy was £20.23, and on this basis, the College was eligible to bid for 28 per cent of Funding Council support, having first deducted the amounts of any vired Hunter Funds, grants or disposal receipts. The Hunter Funds and disposal receipts amounted to 35 per cent of the College's funding target, and it was felt reasonable to hope that an aggregate of around 10 per cent might be achieved in grant support, so the maximum level of FEFC support was therefore calculated against 55 per cent original project cost.

Running cost savings

Another important possibility for funding any accommodation strategy is the running costs savings which should accrue from increased efficiency. Of necessity, the running costs savings will, to some extent, be a forecast, and it is important not to overestimate the potential savings, thus portraying an overly optimistic scenario.

At accommodation strategy state, the **Sheffield College** estimated the running cost savings to be approaching £1.8 million per year, this being the outturn from the FEFC investment appraisal model. These figures were in turn based upon estimated running costs for the new building of £25 per square metre per annum, and £44 per square metre per annum for the existing stock. This later figure was based on an overall summary of property spending within the College accounts for the year in question, and is consistent with general sector norms currently around £55 per square metre.

At the time of writing, the College estimated the annual net saving by the end of implementation of the strategy to be between £950,000 and £1.15 million. Clearly this figure is somewhat lower than that estimated at accommodation strategy stage, and this can be accounted for by the following reasons:

Phase	Project	Construction Value (i.e. inc. of VAT, fees telecoms & furniture)	Maximum FEFC Support
Phase 1	CA 600s Castle Internal Alterations	£509,746	£78,501
Phase 1	LO 300 Loxley Workshops	£413,417	£63,666
Phase 2	CA 701 — Part 1	£810,732	£124,853
Phase 2	NO 400s Norton Internal Alterations	£743,289	£114,467
Phase 2	SE Centre	£4,492,260	£691,808
Phase 3	CA 701 — Part 2	£540,489	£83,235
Phase 3	NO 200 Arts Block new build	£1,822,390	£280,648
Phase 3	NO 300 LRC new build	£1,356,244	£208,862
Phase 4	PX 600 Construction new build	£2,441,239	£375,951
Phase 4	NE Centre — Part 1	£385,899	£59,428
Phase 4	LO600 Wood Lane alterations	£432,993	£66,681
Phase 5	CA 500 Motor Vehicle new build	£501,509	£77,232
Phase 5	NE — Part 2	£904,163	£139,241
Phase 5	Stocksbridge	£426,966	£65,753
Total		£15,781,336	£2,430,326

Table 4.1: Assessment of possible levels of FEFC support

- At accommodation strategy stage, some 51,158 square metres of the estate was to be removed, with a new build programme of 15,540 square metres. The later proposals removed 46,429 metres and have added back slightly more new build at 15,885 square metres;

- The costs calculated at accommodation strategy stage included an element of staffing costs attributable to a property heading. Matters with a bearing on staff costs were then included within the College's overall financial plan, and cannot be counted twice as running cost savings in the accommodation strategy;

- Research has led to more directly attributable property costs to the buildings in question, providing a more accurate overall picture.

Colleges may wish to utilize running cost savings to fund a commercial loan or other arrangement. However, there may be circumstances under which colleges would prefer to aggregate running cost savings as a lump sum component to the funding target — for example, when running cost savings exceed loan requirements for any period, or when the college has returned to surplus and may use this surplus to fund loans.

Clearly, to forecast such savings, a college must know the cost of running existing property and be able to identify the cost of running new buildings. Existing running costs can be identified by reference to college accounts and by researching to build up data. It is worth recalling when doing this exercise that the FEFC, amongst others, estimates older properties to cost approximately double the costs of new buildings.

If running costs savings form an integral part of your accommodation strategy implementation, then the actual realization of these savings is of key financial importance. In developing your financial strategies, it is important to:

- set performance targets for the new building — wherever feasible, this should be a contractual requirement;

- continue to monitor and research the existing costs;

- ensure that there is an appropriate safety margin as each phase is brought forward.

In addition to direct property running costs, the operation of an estate with a lower number of principal and minor sites will inherently be more efficient than one with a greater number. Results will include operational savings not directly attributable to property, for example, staff time and inter–site travel. It is difficult to fully quantify such savings in advance, but, as with property costs, these savings will accrue as each phase of your accommodation strategy is developed, and the savings may be taken as either lump sum contributions to the overall target or as support for loan finance.

Commercial sources

Having explored all the above sources of funding, colleges may still need to fund a remaining deficit from commercial sources. For example, it may be possible to enter into partnership arrangements under the Privates Finance Initiative (PFI), sale and lease back arrangements, straight forward rental opportunities, or any number of more complex strategies.

The key criteria in deciding if commercial sources of finance are a possibility are whether the college can afford the repayments and whether it can obtain the finance. Colleges running at a deficit may be unable to enter into into major unsecured borrowing arrangements, and any simple loan or mortgage arrangements will require security in the form of existing and new property.

If financing the accommodation strategy is difficult and requires the college to enter into major borrowing, the following guidelines may be helpful:

- keep each phase of the strategy discrete, so that it substantially stands alone and the college can stop after any one phase;

- even within phases, there should be opportunities to delay spending on certain projects;

- decisions to proceed with subsequent stages should be dependent upon the success of other funding sources and on an overall recovery plan.

Chapter 5

Phasing of the Strategy

Obviously, when dealing with a multi-million pound accommodation strategy, it will not be possible to do everything at once. College life must go on, students must be able to study in appropriate accommodation, staff must be able to continue their work and, critically, finance must be in place for each element of the strategy.

In many cases, finance for each element of the strategy may be dependent on successful completion of prior projects, so even if it were possible to completely suspend the delivery side of college business for a while, it would still not be possible to implement an accommodation strategy without a gradual phased development plan. When determining how the delivery of the strategy could be phased, the following points must be considered:

- Which buildings can be taken out of use and courses transferred to other sites with little or no modification to the receiving centre?

- Which projects can be done in isolation and are not dependent either on what has happened before or on projects to come later?

- What will be included in each phase? Each phase is likely to contain some alteration/new build and some disposal of property;

- Are all projects within a phase related? All included projects need to be completed within that phase. However, each phase should stand alone, so that gaps between each phase are not necessarily detrimental to the overall strategy;

- If a phase of the strategy is accelerated, which means it overlaps with previous phases, can the college handle all the projects together? Too many projects taking place together could lead to inadequate supervision and potential catastrophe, i.e. projects not being completed on time and insufficient accommodation for timetabled courses;

- Have contingency plans been made to ensure that any delay in the completion of new build or alteration does not lead to students having nowhere to go at the start of their course?

The Sheffield College Experience

Delivering the Sheffield College accommodation strategy presented management with such an enormous task that phasing was absolutely critical to its success. In some cases, it was immediately clear that small buildings, usually annexes, would be taken out of use and courses transferred to other sites with little or no modification to the receiving centre, and simply making better, more efficient use of available space. In such cases, the transfer of courses and staff could take place at almost any time at the beginning of any academic year. A number of such situations were identified and put into Phase One of the strategy.

This enabled the college to take small, usually old and inefficient buildings out of use and sell them off, offering two immediate benefits:

1   Immediately reducing running costs of the estate, i.e. rates, heating, lighting, cleaning, security, caretaking etc;

2   Providing capital which could be ploughed back as pump priming finance for the rest of the strategy;

Once buildings to be closed had been identified, the college looked at where courses could be moved and what modifications/alterations/extensions would be needed to the receiving building. In most cases, several options were possible and options appraisals were carried out, considering curriculum mix, finance, access, and transport.

Once these decisions were made, it became clear what alterations had to be made to which retained buildings before other buildings could be closed. These related projects were then put together within a phase. All projects within a phase had to be carried out in that phase and in the right order, i.e. each phase had to be self–contained. For example, the emptying of Stradbroke — one of the Sheffield College's main sites identified for closure — was reliant on alterations at both Castle and Norton, two other main sites which were to be improved and expanded as part of the accommodation strategy. These projects all formed Phase Two of the strategy.

Some projects could be done in isolation, as they were not dependent on what had gone before or conditional on projects to come later, e.g. the modernization of a neighbourhood centre. Stocksbridge, for example, a neighbourhood centre in a major population centre to the north of the city, was to house existing and future courses in a smaller, more modern unit, more appropriate to present needs. The courses were not transferring into or out of this centre, so this project could stand alone.

All such projects were grouped together in Phase Five, the last phase. Unlike other phases, projects within it could be completed at any stage, brought forward or delayed.

Chapter 6

Consultation

There are many people — both individuals and groups — who should be consulted before firm plans for the future are established. People working in different centres or in different curriculum areas of the college will have useful insights to offer into what is essential and what is not, and may well highlight critical factors which would not necessarily be picked up from the centre.

Planning and implementing an appropriate accommodation strategy for the future is also likely to involve a certain amount of upheaval and change, and it is essential that those involved in or affected by the changes feel some ownership of them, if large scale discontent and non-cooperation is to be avoided. Consultation may involve the following individuals or groups:

Internal
College directors
Centre managers
Accommodation officers
Curriculum groups
Programme and Sector/School managers
Staff
Students
Trade unions
Governors

External
Members of Parliament
Local authority/town council representatives from
appropriate departments, e.g. Education and Planning
Secondary schools
User groups at centres
Associated Professional/Industry bodies
The general public

The Sheffield College Experience

The consultation process around the Sheffield College accommodation strategy included more than 100 meetings during the first
two years with various groups and individuals, and this figure
was likely to double by the end of the third year. Most of the
meetings were informal and focused on how the strategy would
impact at a very local level.

Throughout the consultation, it became clear that (as with
the other ex–public services), the general public's perception is
that the College is still in the 'public domain', and this was a key
factor in designing the extensive public consultation process. Many
of the initial meetings dealt with the feeling that the College was
removing a 'community leisure provision' by closing buildings. In
some instances this was true because of historical relationships
with the local education authority. However, the College was now
seen to have assumed responsibility for the community leisure
activities — even in the eyes of some councillors.

**In designing the method of consultation, the College was
clear that the process was about consultation and not
negotiation. Whilst the results of the process changed and
influenced elements of the strategy, the overall scheme
was not open for debate.**

The consultation process varied in scale, from small community groups meeting in someone's lounge to several hundreds of people attending general public meetings. For some audiences, it was more appropriate to hold meetings with groups but, in other cases, such as MPs, it was felt more appropriate that these should be dealt with individually. Because of the sensitivities and pressures surrounding such meetings, the College felt it was important to carefully select appropriate representatives who would attend most, if not all, of the meetings. **One** lesson learned was that it is important not to underestimate the staff workload and time implications of taking the consultation process seriously.

The consultation process highlighted the fact that the 'community' had loyalties to 'bricks and mortar', even where the quality of the building was in a very poor state and was not particularly well used. Often, the decision to close a centre was not well received, and the College found itself accused of 'rushing into things' when deciding on closures, and of being too slow when making decisions on whether to build new facilities.

By far the most difficult issue to deal with was the relationship between FEFC funding methodology, space utilization and the financing of the accommodation strategy. It was difficult to develop understanding amongst the general public of the fine detail or rationale used by the FEFC, and this was particularly evident in cases where College premises have been used for community or social activities not directly related to education and/or training. Again, because of the perception that the council owned certain properties, politicians became involved in the debate, thus raising the status of the consultation process.

Although the overall aims of the accommodation strategy were to meet the needs of both the College and the city, there were times when it was difficult to convince the general public that the College was not just asset stripping, moving premises into prosperous areas and withdrawing a community service. However, the College's firm commitment to, and investment in, the consultation process has succeeded in raising awareness of the issues involved and building support for the necessary changes.

Internal and External Consultation

The following methods of consultation form part of the Sheffield College's approach.

Internal

- Talk to all staff at each centre to explain draft of strategy;

- Discuss with each curriculum group who may be affected by any change in accommodation, including support staff;

- Internal bulletins to staff to outline plan and procedures;

External

- Outline of strategy seeking comments from HE institutions in Sheffield, secondary school heads, the Training and Enterprise Council, and the Chamber of Commerce;

- Meeting with Sheffield City Council to outline plans;

- Meeting with local councillors in areas where provision was being removed;

- Meeting with MPs representing Sheffield;

- Meeting with the Chairs of the six Community Consultative Committees;

- Meeting with each Community Consultative Committee and User group separately;

- Media releases and briefings.

All meetings and comments were recorded and fed back to the Accommodation Strategy Planning Group for analysis and, where appropriate, built into the Strategy.

Working with the Media

Obviously, the local media provide an important mechanism for communicating with a large number of people quickly and efficiently, and the Sheffield College made the most of the opportunities through a proactive approach to media relations.

During the development and implementation of an accommodation strategy there will be a whole range of issues which could be of interest to the local media including starts on site for building projects, dealing with the challenges of relocation, property sales, opening of new developments, public meetings and new facilities, to mention just a few. Coverage by the local media is not only an important way of letting people know of the organization's plans, but can also be a useful way of generating feedback and opinion from local communities and others affected by change.

Some useful hints for dealing with the media include:

- Make contact with the local journalists who are likely to be covering your stories. By keeping in touch, you are much more likely to be able to put your side of the story;

- When issuing media releases, make sure they are brief, accurate and to the point. Always include contact names and telephone numbers for more information, and make sure that those contact people will be available and are properly briefed to talk to journalists wishing to follow up any stories;

- When issuing a media release, always include a couple of sentences that can be directly used as quotes, so that, if the journalist cannot get hold of anyone directly, the story can still be used as if it were based on a live interview;

- Media briefings can be a useful way of delivering more detailed background information which is necessary to a full understanding of any issue and generating more accurate and useful coverage. However, do not overdo such events — journalists are busy people and do not welcome being called out when there is not a real story for them to follow up;

- Exclusives can be a useful way of ensuring comprehensive coverage of your message in the most appropriate media. For example, if you have an issue relevant to a particular area of the city or region, it can be useful to offer the local paper an exclusive interview. However, you will often want all the local media to carry information, and offering too many exclusives to one outlet can leave others feeling less positive about your organization;

- Target your stories to different specialists within the media — for example a property sale might be of interest to the business editor, whereas the opening of new facilities might be more appropriately directed to the education specialist;

Chapter 7

The Implementation Phase

Once you have considered all aspects of your accommodation strategy, and settled on an acceptable way forward, the next and final stage will be the critical task of implementation. Clearly, this will be of key concern to governors, all members of the college body, all students and clients of the college and, indeed, any individual or group affected by the organization and its operations.

Before embarking on implementation, it is important to identify the key areas which will need to be addressed, and to identify key objectives or risks which will form the priorities during implementation. A comprehensive and integrated implementation plan must be a key priority if the accommodation strategy is to be successful.

Construction and Property Issues

An accommodation strategy is likely to be made up of numerous projects, the realization of which may well involve large numbers of organizations and individuals. Managing this process, and the high levels of expenditure involved will therefore require an exceptional management effort, and a key priority for the college must be to produce a detailed management plan covering these issues.

Issues for consideration under this heading include:

- **Value for Money** — the college must ensure that it gains the best possible value from the significant investment it is planning to make;

- **Quality of Product** — the college must ensure that in expending such large sums it achieves the desired design and specification to meet both its short term requirements and longer term objectives;

- **Core Business** — the college must ensure that both the management task and the physical activity of implementing the Strategy does not impact adversely on its core business, either through unacceptable disruption or through overburdening key staff;

- **Risk** — all construction work carries risk, and the college must take the appropriate steps to minimize this and promote value for money;

- **Control** — the college must ensure that it can exercise the necessary control over:
  - the strategy as a whole as it develops;
  - the individual projects in terms of cost and programme;
  - the design and quality of the built product;

- **Relationships and Credibility** — the implementation of the proposals will require very careful handling of college relationships with both internal and external groups. Furthermore, the college must ensure that its reputation is enhanced rather than damaged by the management of the accommodation strategy process.

Making it Happen

Clear roles and responsibilities must be identified to ensure that construction and property issues are effectively managed. The creation of a management team to oversee and control the implementation is a useful way forward, and membership should include individuals with the necessary skills and experience to carry out the following:

- control of financial aspects;

- co–ordination of internal college groups;

- ongoing estates management;

- project management;

- control of quality of built products;

- keeping the strategy on course

The group could be made up of both internal and external members, depending on the skills, experience and resources available in house.

Key Actions

- Present and explain the build proposals to internal and external groups;

- Initiate planning applications to maximize the value of disposal sites;

- Arrange for the marketing and disposal of these sites;

- Initiate proposals for the closure, demolition and security of properties to close;

- Conclude investigations for new sites and commence commercial negotiations;

- Arrange briefings over the detailed proposals for college groups;

- Initiate designs to planning application stage, then submit and negotiate applications for the new proposals;

- Ensure all detailed proposals remain within the accommodation strategy guidelines;

- Issue tenders for consultant teams and initiate management procedures for the control of project teams;

- Devise procedures for the control of project costs and take all necessary actions;

- Devise procedures to ensure projects remain on programme;

- Set appropriate quality and specification standards and, if necessary, design standards;

- Initiate procedures for vetting the quality of built products;

- Decide upon appropriate procurement routes;

- Where appropriate, establish PFI testing procedures and conduct a programme of PFI negotiations and discussions;

- Continue to liaise with FEFC Property Advisors;

- Arrange for the submission of funding bids to the FEFC and other organizations

Financial Matters

Clearly, this will be an area of very high priority for college managers and governors. Key aspects of this area include:

- Maintaining strict control on project costs;

- Avoiding or minimizing financial risks;

- Seeking maximum value for money in all areas and at every stage;

- Seeking the most beneficial funding package to the college.

Making it Happen

It is important to establish management procedures to maintain tight control of the financial aspects of accommodation strategy implementation, both through regular reporting to both Governors and the Directorate, and by instituting firm procedures for use by the accommodation strategy Management Team during the implementation stages.

Key Actions

- Continue to action project costs and develop greater certainty, particularly during the early phases;

- Begin the disposal and rationalization process to add certainty to a key funding areas and reduce college running costs;

- Continue discussions with FEFC over the financial strategy and its progressive refinement, these discussions to include arrangements for virement of Hunter Funds, where applicable;

- Submit funding bids to FEFC under 95/25;

- Submit grant funding bids to appropriate authorities as early as possible;

- Investigate and refine the appropriate VAT deferment strategy;

- Continue to develop discussions with potential private sector funding partners, leading to the most beneficial loan or finance arrangements;

- Initiate and develop negotiations with PFI operators to seek alternative financial strategies and decide upon the most beneficial route to the college;

- Continue to investigate running costs, particularly those associated with the new properties, and set strict parameters;

- Refine the preferred financial strategy and update on a regular basis;

- Establish procedures for financial controls in all areas, including phase costs, cashflow, and balance sheet implications.

Human Resources Implementation Plan

Human Resources is an issue of key concern when implementing an accommodation strategy. Issues to be addressed are likely to include:

- Identification of staff employed at centres proposed for closure;

- Determination of staffing requirements at proposed new centres and centres which will remain open;

- Vacancies at all centres arising prior to closure may need to be filled on a temporary basis where appropriate;

- The possibility of offering a voluntary release scheme across the college, if necessary, at key dates during the implementation period;

- Redeployment/relocation programme to operate throughout the implementation period;

- Consultation with staff and trade unions on the proposals, human resource implications and potential reductions;

- Planning a timescale for change, acknowledging that the resolution of human resource issues can take a significant amount of time.

Consultation and Dissemination of Information

It is likely that, during the planning period, the college will already have made significant efforts to consult widely and thoroughly over its proposals, both within the college and with external bodies. Nevertheless, if the accommodation strategy is to be successful, this process must continue, and in fact be intensified as projects are brought through to implementation. In addition to seeking consultation, colleges must also ensure relevant information is easily available to all interested parties.

Careful handling of this process is important to:

- Ensure staff and students feel they have a degree of ownership of the strategy;

- Avoid negative impact on morale for staff and students most affected;

- Ensure external groups understand the college's rational and can support the college as it moves to implement the strategy;

- Avoid an adverse impact on recruitment of students;

- Build enthusiasm amongst staff involved in projects, and all staff affected by the strategy;

- Ensure future projects are not jeopardized by bad experiences on the early projects;

- Ensure that prospective students are attracted by the proposed benefits and not discouraged.

Key Actions

- Regular briefings to reach all staff to ensure that they are fully informed of the progress of the accommodation strategy;

- A full briefing summary to be issued to all staff and external interest groups;

- Regular centre–based presentations to explain how the proposals will affect each centre and the timescales;

- Ensure that information about the implementation of the strategy is regularly updated and continually available to all interest groups;

- Proactive use of the local media as a means of dissemination up-to-date information to the widest possible audience;

- Other publicity activity, such as leaflets, posters, public meetings, as appropriate.

Curriculum Issues

Getting the curriculum decisions and relocations right is one of the most challenging but most important parts of your accommodation strategy. At this stage, it is important to firm up any strategic curriculum changes as key strategic decisions on both curriculum areas to be pursued or rationalized in the next few years and how and where some of the curriculum is to be delivered will have a definitive influence on the eventual shape-up of the profile of college accommodation and can certainly contribute to achieving the target efficiency.

There is little doubt that not only will curriculum changes continue to take place, but the pace will also quicken. Because of the speed and complexity of such changes, it will be increasingly difficult to predict the future with any degree of accuracy Any particular type of specialist accommodation will not be suitable for too long. The key here is flexibility, and it is essential that the profile of accommodation introduced is planned and designed with the necessary flexibility to cope with the expected varied and frequent changes of curriculum needs.

After the development of the initial strategic framework, the more detailed development of the profile of accommodation and its implementation in the next stage for each relocated curriculum area will need to rely on the involvement of staff in the specialist subject areas, but will be guided by the college's overall key strategic curriculum direction. **It may be helpful to identify an**

Implementation Team for each of the relocated curriculum areas, consisting of relevant specialist staff and middle managers, to plan and implement the relocation projects.

Key Actions

- Establishment of Implementation Teams for curriculum areas;

- Full coordination with other groups, e.g. centres, key management areas;

- Publication of detailed curriculum proposals with timescales and actions for implementation;

Marketing and Student Recruitment Issues

It is important to take steps to ensure that the college's student recruitment is not damaged by the disruption and relocation which will inevitably arise from the implementation of your accommodation strategy. Effective publicity is critical both in terms of information dissemination and in building support for the developments.

Key Actions

- Local media interest is likely to be high and should be used effectively as part of your communications planning;

- Press releases should be issued regularly and should include positive comment from college governors and managers, local people, local community groups etc, to demonstrate broad-based support for the strategy;

- Plans should be put in place for detailed and timely communication with local and regional careers services and secondary schools;

- Specific plans should be designed to take account of where the strategy is likely to have a particular impact on specific communities;

- Use of other publicity media — such as mail shots, poster campaigns, leaflets — should be actively considered;

- Locations 'at risk' as a result of the strategy should be identified, and appropriate responses put in place — i.e. transportation assistance where students will have to change centres.

Estate Management Issues

The objectives of this part of the implementation process must be:

- To minimize the impact and disruption on the operating estate;

- To achieve the smoothest possible implementation of new projects;

- To control the quality of new buildings with a view to minimizing future running costs and developing uniform standards across the estate;

- To monitor the implemented strategy and bring forward any necessary revisions;

The Estates Manager or equivalent will already be a member of the accommodation strategy Management Team, and will therefore already be involved in many aspects of the process. However, a number of tasks will fall particularly on the Estates Management section, and these are outlined in key actions.

Key Actions

- Participating in arrangements for the closure, demolition, security and disposal of redundant sites;

- Instigating the most appropriate and beneficial on site arrangements for construction projects as they come forward for implementation;

- Managing disruption to existing centres;

- Assisting in making arrangements for the transfer of staff and equipment from centres due to close to their new centres;

- If necessary, as part of the contingency, arranging temporary accommodation to manage the decant programme;

- To continue to maintain the fabric of the buildings identified for closure on a minimum necessary basis;

- If necessary, to advise the Director of Finance of ongoing maintenance costs of properties identified for closure;

- With other managers, co–ordinate all health and safety aspects relating to both existing properties and the new developments, and advise the college on procedures for the CDM regulations;

- To ensure that maintenance work is programmed to derive maximum advantage from the accommodation strategy and vice versa;

Management Overview and Risk Identification

There is no doubt that all of the college's activities will be affected as a result of the implementation of the accommodation strategy, and it is therefore critical that clear and effective management of the strategy is carried out.

Many of the management issues have been addressed under earlier headings in this chapter. However, there is an overriding management objective to the implementation of the strategy, which is to identify, quantify and manage risks by effective formal management techniques.

Key Actions

- To commission a comprehensive risk analysis;

- To ensure that a procedure to allocate and manage risk is implemented;

- To establish a mechanism for contingency management (contingency being the quantified output from the risk analysis)

Risk Identification

From the identification of risks, it is possible to undertake a fully quantified risk analysis using one of the recognized techniques (e.g. MERA). However, you may need to buy in specialist support in order to carry this out effectively.

The types of risk most likely to occur are:

- Modifications to the strategy;

- Development of Design;

- Accuracy of estimates;

- Unforeseen/unpredictable events

Changes to the Strategy

The content of your strategy should have been developed through detailed consultation with key representatives who have expertise in certain areas of college activities, and this content is likely to develop further as consultation continues.

At this stage, you will still be deciding how to implement the proposals, and these decisions could have a bearing on the extent of consultant services and consequently levels of fees. Your funding strategy will almost certainly consist of a number of elements, all of which are as yet not fully fixed or secured, including:

- Virement of Hunter Funds;

- Achievement of disposal receipts;

- Obtaining grant funding

- Obtaining FEFC capital support;

- Achievement of running cost savings;

- Securing commercial loans;

- Management strategies which include the deferment of VAT;

Changes to the rules covering any of the constituent elements of the funding strategy over the life of the strategy are therefore a risk. Changes in interest rates on any commercial loans remain important even though plans for reducing the unpredictability can be implemented.

Your accommodation strategy is likely to be based on current student numbers together with allowances for grants in accordance with the strategic plan. Both changes in the enrolments planned and the make up of type of attendance of those enrolments could alter the content of the projects which make up the overall strategy.

It is important to accept that the strategy may need to develop as the college's financial position and the perceived market need alter.

Development of design

The outline project designs accompanying your strategy are likely to be initial appraisals which will not have had the benefit of detailed investigations. Issues which may still require resolution include:

- Fire strategies;

- Structural requirements where internal alterations have to be made;

- The capacity of central boiler plant to support increased demand and for mechanical and electrical services;

- Specialist design considerations in terms of noise reduction/acoustic design;

- Possible extended planning processes which may adversely affect the programme and cashflow.

Accuracy of estimating

Issues which could affect the accuracy of initial estimating include:

- Ground conditions

- Inflation

- Tender prices

- Fitting out

- Fees

Unforeseen/unpredictable events

A range of unforeseen/unpredictable events which could affect the accommodation strategy include:

- Change in Government — a change of Government and policies towards the construction industry could stimulate the market, resulting in the possibility of rising costs and possibly sales values. A change of Government policies on further education could also have a significant impact on your accommodation strategy;

- Change in planning designation — A change in the current planning designation could affect your strategy;

- Planning Approval Requirements — At this stage, planning applications have not yet been submitted, therefore planning requirements may still be unknown;

- Changes in Building Regulations — Any change in Building Regulations prior to approval being granted may affect the project costs;

- Ground conditions — Geotechnical surveys may highlight problems, such as difficult ground conditions resulting from old mine workings;

- Removal of Contaminated Ground — Ground investigations may reveal ground contamination, which would create extra work and expense;

- Bankruptcy/Insolvency of Contractor or Consultants — If the Main Contractor or Consultants were to become insolvent, there is a risk that to complete the project would costs more money.

- Industrial Action — If the Contractor or other labour involved in the construction or supply of materials were to take industrial action, the programme of work could be delayed with a subsequent increase in costs.

- Variations — If changes are determined by the college at a late stage in the design period, they could have an adverse effect on construction duration and costs;

- Construction Delays — If delay is caused to the Contractors for any reason beyond their control, claims for disruption and expense may arise.

The Sheffield College Experience

The Sheffield College Estates Manager was designated as the person responsible for implementation and its overall project management. An Accommodation Implementation Group was also established to ensure that the strategy was kept on course and that any modifications to it were handled properly. The group was also responsible for ensuring a continued flow of information to staff, carrying out consultation regarding any strategy modifications, and providing advice to Estates Committee from a wider group of managers. The Accommodation Implementation Group also has an overview of the Client Groups' work and project developments.

The membership of the Accommodation Implementation Group included all senior managers originally involved in developing the strategy, as follows:

- Project Manager

- Estates Manager

- Learning Strategies Manager

- Marketing Manager

- Curriculum Manager for Cross College work

- Curriculum Manager for Post-19 work

- One of the four Heads of Schools

- All six Heads of Centre (Chairs of Client Groups)

- Personnel manager

- Management accountant

Client Groups

These were formed for each project within the strategy, and dealt with project details, e.g. size and design of new laboratories, location, size and layout of rooms, etc. For example, the Castle Centre Client Group looked at the details of housing the vocational science and health and social care courses which were to be transferred from the Stradbroke Centre.

- Each Client Group consisted of staff from curriculum areas moving into new accommodation to ensure their needs were met and also any existing curriculum areas whose rooms may be affected by the alterations.

- Chairs of each Client Group were the Heads of receiving centre and were also members of the Accommodation Implementation Group.

- A member of Estates Department attended all Client Group meetings, as did the appointed architects and building contractors at a later stage.

- Client Group took ownership of the project details and worked within the sums of money available for their project.

- Progress on projects was reported back to the Accommodation Implementation group by the Client Group Chairs.

- The Client Groups were also asked to consider contingency planning in the event of projects not being completed on time.

The Estates Committee

The process of managing and coordinating the individual projects within the accommodation strategy requires a clear organization structure.

The Estates Committee deals with all aspects of estates, including the accommodation strategy. The Committee is chaired

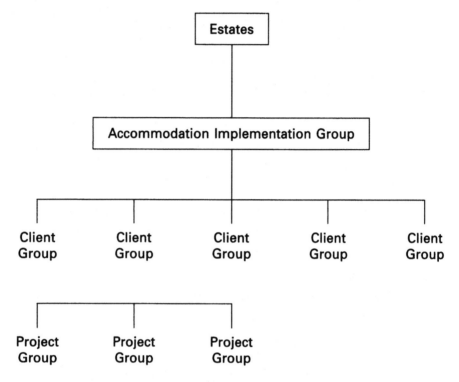

Figure 7.1: The Estates Committee

by the Principal, and also has a Governor as a member. The following groups are responsible for implementing the changes:

1 The College Estates Committee has overall responsibility for the development process;

2 The accommodation strategy Implementation Group is the continuation of the previous Feasibility Study Group and is responsible for the coordination and monitoring of the overall implementation of the strategy;

3 The Human Resources (HR) Group is responsible for the coordination of HR issues which are being managed by

the Client Coordinating Groups, in liaison with Schools/ Divisions and ensuring college-wide consultation with staff and trade unions;

4   The Estates Department is responsible for commission- ing the individual projects from the strategy, providing support for the Client Coordinating and Individual Project Groups, maintaining College Estates management policies and monitoring the performance of the consultants on each commission within the guidelines set by the strategy Implementation Group;

5   The Client Coordinating Group have responsibility for allocation of space, the coordination of individual projects, transfers between Centres and relevant displacement issues. They are also responsible for all HR aspects of the implementation, including consultation and involvement of staff and the implications for staff resources;

6   The Individual Client Project Groups have responsibility for the organization of the space allocated, the design and layout of the areas and the physical movement of staff and equipment in line with the guidelines issues by the strategy Implementation Group. It is recommended that these groups are kept as small as possible, whilst allowing appropriate representation.

Chapter 8

Conclusion

Managing a college's estate is a complex and time consuming business, especially at times of great change in demand for provision. Creating an accommodation strategy which is affordable, robust and yet flexible enough to take account of changing circumstances will take a high level of commitment, planning and initiative for it to be successfully implemented.

Although the Sheffield College is, at the time of writing, still in the process of implementing its accommodation strategy, we hope that our experience so far will prove useful and offer some guidelines for those colleges at an earlier stage of the procedure.

One of the main lessons we have learned is the need for a flexible approach, allowing enough leeway for a rapid response to changing circumstances. Things do not always go according to plan, and it is important that new factors can be incorporated into the overall plan. For example, you may find that grants you had hoped for do not materialize, and have to alter plans accordingly, or you may find that beneficial planning consent could net you sums higher than expected from property sales, and this too can lead to a change of direction.

A combination of in house skills and knowledge topped up by external expertise can help you deliver the accommodation strategy you need for the twenty-first century. An effective and thriving further education sector is vital to the training and education needs faced by Britain as we move towards the next millennium, and the right kind of accommodation strategy is an essential part of our success.

Index

Index

Index

Index

Printed in the United States
by Baker & Taylor Publisher Services